My Wife's Hands

Shikaorsor Ademu-John

My Wife's Hands
An African Cookbook

Table of Contents

Introduction

A chef is usually complimented on the excellence of his or her food by phrases like "my compliments to the chef" or in other circles "it tastes so good, I see you put your foot in it". In Sierra Leone and other parts of West Africa, chefs are complemented by a measure of their hands. Good hands make good food.

My mother had great hands, whenever she cooked all my cousin's fussed over her food. Then I met my wife Rita, she has excellent hands. As the saying goes "a man will most times choose a person with the same attributes as his mother". From Rita I learned the joy and true passion of cooking African dishes. I learned from one of Sierra Leone's finest teachers. A sophisticated lady with great hands, she embodies precision, skill and soul. To watch this goddess move around the kitchen, is to understand what soul food is all about.

The expression "soul food" which today is synonymous with African American cuisine, I think has a deeper meaning that can be traced to African cooking. My view of soul cooking is the preparation of a dish with deep passion, attention, skill and love. When you love the art of cooking, what you cook not only shows in the display of the dish but follows through to the taste of the food. Most restaurants and chefs fuss over presentation. While presentation is a prime factor in food preparation it is of no relevance if the taste of the food is not up to par.

Soul cooking has no definite measurements, it comes with passion and practice. Great cooking is about timing, knowing when and how much is needed at the right time. No sooner, no later only at the right time. Soul cooking is cooking from the heart. A tradition that is well known to the African chef.

My wife is passionate about her food. Most intriguing is the consistency of her dishes. Whenever you can eat the same dish from a cook and it always maintains a consistent taste and flavor every time, that is the first vital sign of a good hand. An intrigue of African cuisine is the aromas that fills the air as it cooks. Hunger is provoked by delicious smells that excite the nostrils, which in turn seduce the taste buds into an inevitable surrender. Resistance is futile as an eventual consumption only leads to an insatiable appetite that can only be satisfied by a full stomach.

I have witnessed time and time again as our children while preoccupied with their video games are drawn by the food's aroma running into the kitchen unsummoned to the dinner table. Good food can be quite powerful. It brings families and friends together. Some times it might even unite adversaries if not for a while at least for a passing moment. Good food affords great company between strangers. The aroma of dishes like, cassava leaves, petehteh leaves, bittas, jollof rice, palm oil stew, to mention a few can pull a child effortlessly away from his or her video world into the dinner table. Various parties and receptions led to our guests scrambling for take-out boxes before the party was over. You always know when the food is great, especially if the food is finished before the end of the reception and the guests are asking for more or if everyone is engaged in a fierce discussion about the cuisine.

While artists bring life to a canvas, a chef's masterful collage begins in the kitchen and then spreads out to the dinner table. The enticing presentation once visually consumed is then ingested through our taste buds where it creates an indelible mark that conjures memories of flavors, events, places and people. Like good food, good hands can become the hallmark of a successful occasion and are never forgotten.

There is a strong connection between African food, American soul food, Spanish, Portuguese and Indian cuisines that I beleive date back to the slave trade. This connection is most times misunderstood because we fail to see and relate to the relocation of our ancestors as they were displaced and migrated to different parts of the world. It is my guess that as the slaves were brought over from Africa, they may have traveled with some of their food products and or plant seeds.

Upon arrival whatever was saved was planted and other food items were substituted with similar plants and vegetables found here in America or their other ports of entry.

There are so many common ground dishes that are identical on both the African and the American continent. For instance Black eye peas are also known as Bench (in Sierra Leone), Hopping John (Southern America) or Red red (Ghana). Another example is collard greens usually substituted for bitter leaves. Furthermore, the similarity with petehteh leaves soup and the Indian lamb saag dish. There is evidence that there is a strong similarity between our foods across ethnic borders. As West Indians consume rice and beans, Latin families enjoy rice also with beans. The same can be said for Indians as they consume rice and peas. Their African brethren enjoy jollof rice and black eye peas or red red as it is called in Ghana.

Sierra Leone where I was born is well known for its mineral wealth especially diamonds. In my opinion, Africa's most precious jewels are its diet and delicious foods. Many of the major ingredients in African dishes have been found to be major contributors to increased medical health. Such ingredients include palm oil, cassava, peanut butter, cayenne pepper etc. Some of the vital and major contributions of the various ingredients are noted in this book, especially since health preservation is a growing global concern today.

While we intend to stage and display some of our favorite dishes in West Africa, we also hope to dispel most of the doubts, myths and unfounded rumors about the nutritional properties and contribution of African foods to a healthy, safe and nutritionally beneficial diet.

As a diabetic myself, my love and insatiable appetite for our food has forced me to examine the properties of its ingredients for safe consumption and a continued promotion of good health. For example in the Malaysian Palm Oil Council's website, palm oil is quoted as being God's gift to the human race. In my opinion, an African diet like most diets around the world will in concert with proper medical monitoring, proper portions and adequate exercise promote good health and an excellent quality of life.

West African dishes are found throughout the continent of Africa under different names because of the variety of dialects spoken throughout Africa. Most times the same dish may also have different names within the same region in the same country. As we illustrate the various dishes in this book we will state some of the names by which they are known in other countries throughout Africa and beyond.

Most of the ingredients listed can be obtained from most local African grocery stores, Asian markets or sometimes a local Spanish grocery store. In case you cannot find one in your state or country, please notify us via e-mail at awujohenterprises@gmail.com and we will assist you in locating the ingredients you may need.

Let us begin with the basic foundation to most of West Africa's vegetable soups and stews. We do not call them vegetable soups, they are commonly known as plasas aka palavasauce. The main ingredient by which the soup is named is usually a plant leaf for example cassava leaves, potato leaves etc. The main sauce that is the foundation to most of these stews and soups is called Alakpah. The alakpah is a concoction of palm oil cooked with onions, spices, herbs and seasonings with a slight variation from one dish to another.

Alakpah Sauce

Alakpah sauce is the main base to most of our vegetable stews or as we call them Palava sauce (a vegetable soup). If one can master the cooking of the Alakpah sauce, you have accomplished a good forty five to fifty percent of cooking the Palava sauce dish of your choice.

The Alakpah is a palm oil based sauce cooked with finely blended Spanish or yellow onions, sweet peppers and an array of herbs and seasonings depending on the locale one is in. In Sierra Leone and parts of West Africa, we utilize the following ingredients.

Ingredients

1. Palm oil
2. Onions
3. Sweet Peppers
4. Salt
5. Black Pepper
6. All purpose seasoning
7. Seasoned salt
8. Water
9. Hot Peppers
   (Habanero or Cayenne)

Preparation

Place a 12 quart saucepan on the stove
Add four cups of water and two cups of palm oil
Bring the palm-oil and water to a boil
Chop six onions, three sweet peppers
Place them in a blender, blend with a half cup of water
Add mixture to the pot
Add a half teaspoon of salt
Add two tablespoons of black pepper
Add one tablespoon of all purpose seasoning
Add two tablespoons of seasoned salt
Depending on your tolerance for heat add one habanero or a half teaspoon of cayenne pepper
Cover the pot and let it continue to boil for 15-20 minutes
Stir consistently to loosen the onions as you cook
Taste as you cook to ensure consistency and season to your liking
Under low heat, continue to simmer for an additional five to ten minutes
For a thicker Alakpah sauce add an additional blended onions and sweet pepper mixture
If a habanero pepper was added, remove from sauce or blend into sauce for a spicier sauce
Serve with rice, foofoo or eba

Serves approximately 8-10 people

Cassava Leaves
Saka Saka

A delectable tasting stew, Cassava Leaves is a mixture of finely grated leaves of the Yucca aka Cassava plant, cooked in a palm oil based sauce with herbs and seasonings until as we say in Africa it is dry (meaning it is almost completely void of excess water).

In some parts of West Africa, especially Sierra Leone, one of the most vital ingredients of Cassava Leaves is the smoked fish (preferably dried Barracuda fish). This particular item is vital because it lends the smoke flavor from the drying process of the fish to accentuate the unique flavor that permeates the finished product.

Ingredients

1. Palm oil
2. Grated Cassava Leaves
3. Water
4. Smoked Dried Fish
   (Barracuda, Kinney or Stalk Fish)
5. Creamy Peanut Butter
6. Salt
7. Black Pepper
8. Seasoned Salt
9. All purpose seasoning
10. Onions
11. Sweet Peppers
12. Beef, Chicken, Pork or Fish as preferred

Preparation

Place a 12 quart saucepan on the stove
Add four cups of water and two cups of palm oil
Bring the palm-oil and water to a boil
Chop six onions, three sweet peppers
Place them in a blender, blend with a half cup of water
Add the mixture to the pot
Add a half teaspoon of salt
Add two tablespoons of black pepper
Add one tablespoon of all purpose seasoning
Add two tablespoons of seasoned salt
Take two Kinney or one chunk of Barracuda fish, remove skin and bones, rinse and add the dried fish to the pot
Add two 16 oz. packets of Cassava Leaves to the pot
Stir consistently as you cook
(Note: The Cassava leaves needs to boil until the leaves are fine and soft. Add water as needed to accomplish this effect, a half cup at a time)
Cover the pot and let it continue to boil for 15-20 mnutes
Add meats as desired within fifteen minuets of boiling
(Note: Beef takes longer to tenderize than chicken. Pay close attention to the tenderness of your meats and remove meats if desired tenderness is acquired)
Taste as you cook and add seasoning to your liking
Under low heat, simmer for an additional 15 minutes
Once the leaves are fine or a smooth taste is acquired, add two 18 oz. bottles of creamy peanut butter and stir it into the cassava leaf mix
Simmer for an additional 10-15 minutes until the dish is thick
Serve over white rice
Serves approximately 8-10 people

Bitter Leaves
Egusi Soup/Onugbo/Ewuro/Shiwaka

As the name implies, the taste of this vegetable is slightly bitter. In its preparation the leaves are washed as needed and most of the bitterness is squeezed out and neutralized with water.

The balance in Bitter Leaves soup is to preserve its healing properties which are mainly contained in its bitterness through its ingredients, while strategically enhancing the leaf's flavor with the soup's other ingredients. The optimal result is a slightly bitter-sweet taste engulfed in the aroma of smoked fish, spices and seasonings.

Ingredients

1. Bitter Leaves
2. Palm Oil
3. Smoked Fish
   (Barracuda, Kinney or Stalk Fish)
4. Grated Egusi seeds
5. Hot peppers
   (Habanero or cayenne)
6. Water
7. Seasoned salt
8. All purpose seasoning
9. Black pepper
10. Boullion cubes
11. Onions
12. Sweet peppers
13. Beef, Chicken, Pork or Fish as preferred

Preparation

Soak two packets of Bitter leaves in a bowl of cold water to wash off the bitter taste
Rinse and strain the soaked leaves with a fine strainer at least twice
Place the strained leaves in a bowl to the side
Place a 12 quart saucepan on the stove
Add four cups of water and two cups of palm oil
Bring the palm-oil and water to a boil
Chop six onions, three sweet peppers
Place them in a blender, blend with a half cup of water
Add the mixture to the pot
Add a half teaspoon of salt
Add two tablespoons of black pepper
Add one tablespoon of all purpose seasoning
Add two tablespoons of seasoned salt and two bouillon cubes
Take two Kinney or one chunk of Barracuda fish, remove skin and bones, rinse and add the dried fish to the pot
Add Bitter leaves to the pot and let it boil for 15-20 mnutes
Add meats as desired within additional fifteen minuets of boiling
(Note: Beef takes longer to tenderize than chicken. Pay close attention to the tenderness of your meats and remove meats if desired tenderness is acquired)
Cover the pot and continue to cook under a medium to high flame for 15-20 minutes
Depending on your tolerance for heat add hot peppers
Stir consistently as you cook while observing the sauce in the pot to obtain a smooth and fine taste of the leaves
Add three 8 oz. packets of grated egusi to the pot and lower the fire
Allow the mixture to cook for at least 20-25 minutes while stirring consistently to ensure adequate balance of spices until the dish is thick
Serve over rice or foofoo, eba or gari
Serves approximately 8-10 people

Krain Krain
Jute Leaves/Obiatah/Palavasauce

A hearty blend of this richly green vegetable in a thick Palm oil Alakpah sauce opens the pallets to one of Africa's well kept jewels. A secret jewel one will agree has long been kept too silent. An exotic, tasty, delicious, green vegetable.

Ingredients

1. Krain Krain/Jute Leaves
2. Palm oil
3. Smoked Dried Fish

   (Barracuda, Kinney or Stalk Fish)
4. Salt
5. Black pepper
6. Water
7. Bouillon cube
8. Onions
9. Sweet peppers
10. Ogiri (if available)
11. Seasoned Salt
12. All purpose seasoning
13, Hot Pepper

   (Habanero or Cayenne)

Note: Ogiri is fermented sesame seeds used for flavoring and added taste. It can be purchased from your local African store. It is not critical to the taste of the dish.

Preparation

Place a 12 quart saucepan on the stove
Add four cups of water and two cups of palm oil
Bring the palm-oil and water to a boil
Chop six onions, three sweet peppers
Place them in a blender, blend with a half cup of water
Add the mixture to the pot
Add a half teaspoon of salt and two tablespoons of black pepper
Add one tablespoon of all purpose seasoning
Add two tablespoons of seasoned salt
Take two Kinney or one chunk of Barracuda fish, remove skin and bones, rinse and add dried fish to the pot
Depending on your tolerance for heat add one habanero or a half teaspoon of cayenne pepper
Cover the pot and let it continue to boil for 15-20 minutes
Stir consistently to loosen the onions as you cook
Add meats as desired within fifteen minuets of boiling
(Note: Beef takes longer to tenderize than chicken. Pay close attention to the tenderness of your meats and remove meats if desired tenderness is acquired)
Taste as you cook to ensure consistency and season to your liking
Under low heat, continue to simmer for an additional five to ten minutes
If a habanero pepper was added, remove or blend into sauce for a spicier sauce
In another pot, place the frozen krain krain/ jute leaves with half a cup of water and place under medium to low heat
Bring the pot to a boil, stiring the leaves as you cook to loosen them
Cook for approximately 10-15 minutes or until the mixture is thick and gooey
Serve by mixing a portion of the sauce to a portion of the leaves
This mixing of leaves to sauce derives the name Obiatah
Eat with rice, foofoo, eba or just plain by itself
Serves approximately 8-10 people

Okra Soup

Okra is a rich blend of Palm oil, blended onions, herbs, seasonings, and spices cooked in an uncovered pot to preserve the slimy draw of the Okra. For best results, blend half of the Okra to be used and chop the other half.

Ingredients

1. Chopped Okra
2. Palm oil
3. Onions
4. Sweet peppers
5. Smoked Dried Fish

   (Barracuda, Kinney or Stalk Fish)
6. Hot Peppers

   (Habanero or Cayenne)
7. Black pepper
8. Seasoned salt
9. All purpose seasoning
10. Water
11. Salt
12. Beef, Chicken, Pork or Fish as preferred

Preparation

Chop one pound of okra, blend one additional pound of okra
Place a 12 quart saucepan on the stove
Add four cups of water and two cups of palm oil
Bring the palm-oil and water to a boil
Chop six onions, three sweet peppers
Blend them with a half cup of water and add to the pot
Add a half teaspoon of salt and two tablespoons of black pepper
Add one tablespoon of all purpose seasoning
Add two tablespoons of seasoned salt
Take two Kinney or one chunk of Barracuda fish, remove skin and bones, rinse and add dried fish to the pot
Depending on your tolerance for heat add one habanero or a half teaspoon of cayenne pepper
Cover the pot and let it continue to boil for 15-20 minutes
Stir consistently to loosen the onions as you cook
Add meats as desired within 15 minutes of boiling
(Note: Beef takes longer to tenderize than chicken. Pay close attention when cooking and remove meats if desired tenderness is acquired)
Taste as you cook to ensure consistency and season to your liking
Under low heat, continue to simmer for an additional five to ten minutes
Once sauce is slightly thickened, add the chopped and blended okra and leave the pot uncovered
Closing the pot will prevent the okra from being deliciously slimy
Simmer under low fire while consistently mixing for 10-15 minutes or until the okra chunks are soft and tender
If a habanero pepper was added, remove or blend into sauce for a spicier sauce
Serve with white rice, foo foo or eba

Serves approximately 8-10 people

Potato Leaves
Petehpeh Leaf/Pehmawu

A delectable blend of the leaves from the sweet potato plant or chopped spinach (either fresh or frozen), cooked in palm oil sauce with beef, fish or chicken as preferred. The sweet unique flavor of this dish is pronounced with the use of creamy peanut butter slow cooked to perfection allowing all the spices and ingredients to perfectly blend. Enticingly delicious!

Ingredients

1. **Potato Leaves**
   or Chopped Spinach
2. **Palm oil**
3. **Smoked Dried Fish**
   (Barracuda, Kinney or Stalk Fish)
4. **Sweet peppers**
4. **Black pepper**
5. **Salt**
6. **Seasoned salt**
7. **All purpose seasoning**
8. **Onions**
9. **Creamy Peanut Butter**
10. **Beef Chicken or fish as desired**

Preparation

Wash and chop three pounds of sweet potato leaves or spinach
Place a 12 quart saucepan on the stove
Add four cups of water and two cups of palm oil
Bring the palm-oil and water to a boil
Chop six onions, three sweet peppers
Place them in a blender, blend with a half cup of water and add to pot
Add a half teaspoon of salt and two tablespoons of black pepper
Add one tablespoon of all purpose seasoning
Add two tablespoons of seasoned salt
Take two Kinney or one chunk of Barracuda fish, remove skin and bones, rinse and add dried fish to the pot
Cover the pot and let it continue to boil for 15-20 mnutes
Add meats as desired within fifteen minuets of boiling
(Note: Beef takes longer to tenderize than chicken. Pay close attention while cooking and remove meats if desired tenderness is acquired)
Note that the onions become sweeter as it cooks, therefore taste as you cook to prevent over seasoning
Under low heat, continue to simmer for an additional five to ten minutes
Once sauce is slightly thickened, add the chopped sweet potato or spinach leaves
Simmer under low fire while consistently mixing for 10-15 minutes
Add two 18 oz. bottles of creamy peanut butter and stir it into the potato leaves mixture
With the pot partially covered, lower the fire to low or medium and cook for about 15-20 minutes or untill sauce gets thicker
Dig in. Serve over rice, foofoo eba or Gari (Grated Yucca)

Serving approximately 8-10 people

Groundnut Soup

Peanut butter soup/Mafeh/Granat Soup

Peanut butter soup is a quick and easy dish that releases a mouth watering aroma that permeates the room and draws everyone to the dinner table. No more formal announcements for dinner!

Ingredients

1. Onions
2. Tomatoes
3. Tomato paste
4. Seasoned salt
5. Salt
6. Black pepper
7. Water
8. Creamy peanut butter
9. Beef, Chicken or Fish
10. Sweet peppers
11. Habanero peppers
12. Thyme
13. Bouillon cube
14. All purpose seasoning

Preparation

Place a 10 quart saucepan on the stove with six cups of water
Chop four onions, two sweet peppers, two tomatoes and add to pot
Place four teaspoons of tomato paste in the pot
Add two tablespoons of seasoned salt
Add half a teaspoon of all purpose seasoning and salt
Add one teaspoon of black pepper and thyme
Add two bouillon cubes
Depending on your tolerance for heat add one habanero pepper
Bring the mixture in the pot to a boil
Cook for approximately 20 minutes
Taste as you go to ensure your seasoning tolerance
Add meats as desired
(Note: Beef takes longer to tenderize than chicken. Pay close attention when cooking and remove meats if desired tenderness is acquired
Fish should not be added at this time, if desired add fish at the end so that it will not overcook)
Pay close attention to the habanera pepper if you like it spicy then allow the pepper to boil until it bursts in the pot, otherwise remove it at least 10-25 minutes into cooking
Once meat is tender add one 18 oz. jar of creamy peanut butter and stir into the mixture, reduce heat to low flame
Do not cover the pot after you add the peanut butter, cook with the pot open
NOTE: The soup will thicken as you cook because of the peanut butter. Pay attention to the amount of peanut butter as per your liking. For a thicker soup, add more tablespoons of peanut butter. If the end result is too thick, just add a half cup of water at a time and boil until it loosens to your desired consistency.
Turn off the fire after 10-15 minutes
Serve over rice, cous cous, boiled cassava, cooked plantains or eat plain

Serves approximately 8-10 people

Pehpeh Soup
Boil soup/Inkrakrainwoing

A staple food throughout most of West Africa. It is similar to the Spanish Mondongo soup (Sopa de mondongo). Pehpeh soup is usually prepared spicy and hot.

Pehpeh soup is actually the base of Groundnut soup aka Peanut butter soup. Most times the only varying ingredients are potatoes, vegetables etc. Okra and the type of meats or fish are added as per your liking. Giving all the different ways pehpeh soup can be prepared, this is my favorite way

Ingredients

1. Onions
2. Tomatoes
3. Tomato paste
4. Seasoned salt
5. Salt
6. Black pepper
7. Water
8. Meats or Fish as desired
9. Sweet peppers
10. Hot Peppers
    (Habenero or cayenne)
11. Thyme
13. All purpose seasoning
14. Bouillon cubes

Preparation

Place a 10 quart saucepan on the stove with six cups of water
Chop four onions, two sweet peppers, two tomatoes and add to pot
Place four teaspoons of tomato paste in the pot
Add two tablespoons of seasoned salt
Add half a teaspoon of all purpose seasoning and salt
Add one teaspoon of black pepper and thyme
Add two bouillon cubes
Add 1-2 habanero peppers or 1 tablespoon of cayenne pepper
(Depending on your tolerance for heat!!!)
Bring the mixture in the pot to a boil
Cook for apporoximately 20 minutes
Taste as you go to ensure your seasoning tolerance
Add meats as desired
(Note: Beef takes longer to tenderize than chicken. Pay close attention when cooking and remove meats if desired tenderness is acquired
Fish should not be added at this time, if desired add fish at the end so that it will not over cook)
Pay close attention to the habanera pepper If you like it spicy then allow the pepper to boil until it bursts in the pot, otherwise remove it at least 10-25 minutes into cooking
Allow to cook for an extra 10-15 minutes or until meat is tender adding half a cup of water as needed to maintain stock
(Note: If meats like beef, goat or fowl (i.e.: hen) are desired, we recommend that they are boiled separately in seasoned water with salt, and black pepper until desired softness is attained. Then add to the soup mixture and cook for about five minutes. Tough or hard meats like goat or beef take a longer time to cook)
Serve with boiled yams, cassava/yuca, potatoes or plantains

Serves approximately 8-10 people

African Stew Soup

African Stew soup is unique than most stews based on the way it is prepared. The various ingredients, herbs, seasonings and spices that collectively simmer to create this delicious staple each echo it's own flavor as they sort through your taste buds. **Relishing!!!**

Note: The secret to an even wholesome taste is a low to medium fire. A slow fire allows the medley of seasonings, spices, and meats to permeate each other effectively..

Ingredients

1. Onions
2. Tomatoes
3. Sweet peppers
4. Thyme
5. Black Pepper
6. Seasoned salt
7. Tomato paste
8. Scallions
9. Olive or Vegetable oil
10. All purpose seasoning
11. Chicken, Beef or Fish as desired

Preparation

Place a 14 inch deep skillet on the stove
Add two cups of olive or vegetable oil, turn heat to low flame (this is to prevent the oil from over heating)
Chop and blend four onions, and two sweet peppers with one cup of water and add slowly into the pot with oil
Add one tablespoon of black pepper and all purpose seasoning
Add two tablespoons of seasoned salt and a half teaspoon of salt
Add one tablespoon of thyme
Add four teaspoons of tomato paste
Stir ingredients in the pot into an even mix and cook for 15-20 minutes
Taste as you cook to ensure proper seasoning
(Note: The onion initially will overpower the mixture with a slightly bitter, sour taste. Allow the mixture to slow cook and you will realize that the mixture will get tastier as the onions release their own sugars)
While the mixture is cooking, slice two onions in long strips, dice one sweet pepper, two tomatoes and one bunch of scallion
Once the mixture begins to fry, add the sliced onions and diced sweet pepper, tomatoes and scallions to the pot
Stir consistently as it cooks for approximately five to ten minutes untill onions and peppers are cooked
Simultaneously, prepare your choice of meat (chicken, beef or fish)
Cut into small pieces and season with a part of seasoned salt, black pepper and salt (Make sure there is no excess water on meat before seasoning)
Fry the seasoned chicken or fsh in a seperate pot with oil of choice
I highly suggest not to fry the meat too dry but juicy at least until there appears to be no bloody juice in the meat
If using beef, boil in a seperate pot until desired tenderness is acquired
Add the cooked meat to the stew in the deep skillet as it cooks under a low fire. for five to ten minutes.
Serve with white or jallof rice (Serves approximately 4-6 people)

Jollof Rice
Red Rice

This delicious rice dish is quite popular throughout West Africa. Different grains of rice can be utilized in preparing this dish. However, we highly recommend that long grain rice is used. A rice dish so delicious that you can eat it by itself.

When cooked with long grain rice, the Jollof rice dish attains its best flavor ever. It is aesthetically pleasing because the grains are almost always loose and a long grain rice absorbs the seasoning and spices that uniquely distinguish Jollof rice from any other.

Ingredients

1. Long grain rice
2. Tomato Paste
3. Black Pepper
4. Salt
5. All purpose seasoning
6. Thyme
7. Boullion cubes
   (If vegetarian, leave this out)
8. Seasoned salt
9. Sweet peppers
10. Olive or vegetable oil
11. Water
12. Onions

Preparation

Place one cup of olive or vegetable oil in a 12 quart saucepan
Blend three chopped onions, four tablespoons of tomato paste, two sweet peppers and two boullion cubes with a half cup of water
Pour the blended mixture slowly into the pot
Bring to a boil and stir consistently as it simmers
Add three tablespoons of seasoned salt
Add one tablespoon of black pepper
Add two tablespoons of thyme
Add one teaspoon of salt
Add one tablespoon of all purpose seasoning
Let the mixture simmer for 10-15 minutes under medium fire
Allow enough time for the onion to yield its own sweetness
Add four cups of water, taste and add seasoning to your liking
Cover the pot and bring to a boil
Add two cups of long grain rice
Mix the rice into the boiling sauce to ensure a balanced blend and coloring of the rice
Cover the pot tightly, if available place a sheet of aluminum foil over the pot's rim before covering the pot. This promotes the mixture to steam faster allowing the rice seeds to cook adequately and evenly
After approximately three to four minutes, lower the fire from medium or high to low. Keep the flame as low as possible and refrain from opening the pot ahead of time
Allow the contents to cook under a low flame for at least 25 minutes (Note: this time may vary depending on the brand of rice that you use)
Serve as desired with stew or vegetables

Serving size 8-10 people

Palm Oil Fry Stew

The unique flavor of palm oil sets the bar higher in this concoction to create a tasty, healthy and exotic stew. Palm oil stew is usually cooked with smoked fish. Over time other meats have been substituted to accommodate new trends on the dinner table and in the market place. This dish can be cooked with vegetables or with fried chunks of fish.

Ingredients

1. Croaker Fish, or fish of your choice
2. Onions
3. Black Pepper
4. Seasoned Salt
5. Garlic
6. Salt
7. Cayenne pepper
8. Palm Oil
9. Sweet peppers
10. Thyme
11. All purpose seasoning

NOTE:
Palm oil may errupt under high pressure or heat by itself. Cook under medium to low heat. Try always to cook with authentic natural Palm oil.

Preparation

Pour two cups of palm oil into a 12 inch deep skillet under medium to low heat

Lightly season cuts of fish (traditionally snapper, croaker or tilapia fish are used for this stew)

Rub in a pinch of seasoned salt, black pepper, garlic powder and cayenne pepper into the fish

Place the cuts of fish in the pan on one side and fry for at least five minutes or until the outer skin looks crispy

Flip the cuts of fish to the other side and fry for another five minutes or until the outer skin is crispy or as desired

Remove the fried fish and place on a plate to the side

Chop and blend four onions and two sweet peppers with one cup of water and add slowly into the pot with palm oil

Add one tablespoon of black pepper and all purpose seasoning

Add two tablespoons of seasoned salt and a half teaspoon of salt

Add one tablespoon of thyme

Stir ingredients in the pot and cook for 15-20 minutes

While the mixture is cooking, slice two onions in long strips and dice one sweet pepper

Once the mixture begins to fry, add the sliced onions and diced sweet peppers

Stir consistently as it cooks for approximately five to ten minutes untill onions and peppers are cooked

Place the Palm oil fried fish in the sauce

Cover the pot and allow to simmer for at least five minutes

Serve over rice, yams, or couscous

Serves apporximately 8-10 people

Couscous

Couscous is indigenous to Northern Africa. It is usually consumed in countries like Morocco and Egypt. However throughout Africa the dish has found a place on the dinner table cooked in a variety of ways.

Couscous can be prepared as a side dish accompanied with a stew and vegetables. It can also be used to garnish a main course or prepared in a delicious mix as a Vegetarian dish. This dish can be prepared in an eclectic combo reminiscent of the Spanish paella featuring a blend of poultry, meats, and seafood which in Sierra Leone is called wan-pot aka one-pot meaning all ingredients in one dish.

Ingredients

1. Couscous
2. Tomato Paste
3. Black Pepper
4. Salt
5. All purpose seasoning
6. Thyme
7. Garlic
8. Seasoned salt
9. Sweet peppers
10. Olive or vegetable oil
11. Water
12. Onions

Preperation

Place four tablespoons of olive or vegetable oil in a 8 quart saucepan
Blend two chopped onions, two tablespoons of tomato paste, one sweet pepper with a half cup of water
Pour the blended mixture slowly into the pot
Bring to a boil and stir consistently as it simmers
Add two tablespoons of seasoned salt
Add one tablespoon of black pepper, all purpose seasoining and thyme
Add a half teaspoon of salt
Let the mixture simmer for 10-15 minutes under medium fire
Chop two onions, one sweet pepper and two garlic cloves and add to pot
Allow enough time for the onion to yield its own sweetness
Add two cups of water, taste and add seasoning to your liking
Cover the pot and bring to a boil
Add two cups of cous cous
At this time if so desired, you may add your choice of cooked seafood or poultry to the pot
Mix the cous cous into the boiling sauce to ensure a balanced blend and coloring of the grain
Cook for approximately five to eight minutes under low fire
Continuously mix the ingredients gently, taste to ensure the cous cous is soft and delectible
If the grains are not soft, sprinkle 1/4 cup of water into the pot and continue to cook until the grain is soft.
Once the grain is soft, cover the pot and turn the flame off.
Allow the pot to sit for three to five minutes
Serve as desired with stew or vegetables

Serving size 6-8 people

Beanch
Black Eye Peas

A unique blend of the African Alakpah sauce with black eye peas in an eclectic blend of spices, seasonings and herbs. This dish can be prepared with a vegan touch or with meats and fish as desired.

Ingredients

1. Black eye peas
2. Onions
3. Palm Oil
4. Seasoned salt
5. Black pepper
6. Garlic
7. Salt
8. Water
9. Sweet peppers
10. All purpose seasoning

NOTE:
Palm oil may errupt under high pressure or heat by itself. Cook under medium to low heat. Try always to cook with authentic natural Palm oil.

Preparation

Place an 8 quart pot with 6 cups of water under high heat
Add one 16 oz. packet of black eye peas
Bring to a boil and allow to cook in a covered pot until the beans are soft (If beans are not soft continue to add 1/4 cup of water to the pot until the beans are soft and water has evaporated)
Place a 10 quart saucepan on the stove
Add one cup of Palm oil under low heat
Chop and blend four onions and two sweet peppers with one cup of water and add slowly into the pot with palm oil
Add one tablespoon of black pepper and all purpose seasoning
Add two tablespoons of seasoned salt and a half teaspoon of salt
Stir ingredients in the pot and cook for 15-20 minutes
Stir consistently as water evaporates and mixture begins to fry
Chop one sweet pepper and add into the sauce
Allow sauce to simmer for five to ten minutes under medium to low heat
Mix the cooked black eye peas with the Palm oil sauce
Serve
Serves apporximately 10 people

Olehleh
Moi Moi

A delicacy made with black eye peas flavored and colored with Palm oil. A bite of this jewel reveals a unique, exotic taste that is deliciously African.

Ingredients

1. Black eye peas
2. Palm Oil or Vegetable oil (Depending on which kind of Olehleh you are making)
3. Seasoned salt
4. Garlic powder
5. White pepper
6. Black pepper
7. Salt
8. Baked or steamed boneless fish (preferably blue Fish or any fish of your liking)
9. Onions
10. Sweet pepper
11. Hot Pepper (Habenero or Cayenne)

Note: Palm oil is used for the red olehleh and vegetable oil is used for the white olehleh as displayed in the picture

Preparation

Place three cups of black eye peas in a bowl of water for about 10-12 hours. Peel off the skin of the black eye peas and strain all skins off the bowl leaving only the white peas
In order to avoid this extensive work, search for peeled beans or de-skinned black eye peas
Season and cook the boneless fish at this time and keep to the side
Blend peeled or cleaned peas with two tablespoons of water
Place blended peas in a bowl
Place a 14 quart saucepan on the stove, fill with 8 quarts of water and bring to a boil
Chop and blend two onions, one sweet pepper with a half cup of water
If spice is preferred add one habanero or a half teaspoon of cayenne
Add the onion and sweet pepper mixture to the blended peas
Cut the cooked fish into chunks and add to mixture
Add two tablespoons of garlic powder and seasoned salt
Add half a teaspoon of salt and white pepper
Add one tablespoon of black pepper
Add one cup of palm oil or vegetable oil
Stir to obtain an evenly colorful mixture. The mixture given the portion of peas to palm oil should be relatively thick but not too liquid
Taste periodically and add seasonings as needed to your liking
Using aluminum foil paper about 8-10 inches square, fold the aluminum squares into a funnel closing all ends but one side where the mixture will be poured
Pour one cup of the mixture into the funnel and seal all sides
Place the folded foil packets into the pot of boiling water and boil for 45-60 minutes.
Remove the aluminum containers from the pot
Allow containers to cool for about 10-15 minutes
Carefully open the folded container and serve the olehleh snack
One packet serves two people

Beans Akara
Black Eye Pea Fritters

The true art of delicacy is tested in the preparation of this dish. Not only does the mixture demand an intricate balance, its application in cooking requires a harmonic release of the mixture into the pan that is only perfected with practice. Good hands are achieved with practice and persistence.

Ingredients

1. Black eye peas
2. Olive oil or vegetable oil
3. Salt
4. White pepper

Note:
Beans akara is usually eaten with a sauce. The recipe for this sauce can be found on page 39.

Preparation

Place a 16 oz. packet of black eye peas in a bowl of hot water
After thirty to fourty minutes rub the beans against each other and remove the skin leaving only the white peas
In order to avoid this extensive work, search for peeled beans or de-skinned black eye peas
Blemd peeled or cleaned peas with two tablespoons of water
Place blended peas in a bowl
Add one tablespoon of salt
Add a half teaspoon of white pepper
Whisk the mixture until it is light and fluffy
Place two cups of olive or vegetable oil in a 10 inch frying pan and heat under medium fire for five to ten minutes
Using your fingers, scoop up a small portion of the blended mixture and release in the forms of balls into the hot oil
Repeat this step until the pot is full with akara balls
If you prefer, use a teaspoon to assist you until you become accustomed to using your fingers
Using a fork control the balls of bean fritters as they cook to a golden brown color
Remember a thicker mixture allows you more control
Revmove from the pan and place on a plate and allow to cool for five to ten minutes

Serves approximately 10 people

Rice Akara Balls
Banana Balls/Banana Fritters/Akaraje

A very tasty snack that wins the hearts of children and grown ups alike. A delicate blend of over ripe bananas in a mixture with brown sugar, cinnamon, nutmeg and rice flour that can only make for good conversation and company.

Ingredients

1. Ripe bananas
2. Rice flour
3. Nutmeg
4. Olive or vegetable oil
5. Brown sugar
6. Cinnamon

Note:
Rice akara is usually eaten with a sauce. The recipe for this sauce can be found on page 39.

Preparation

Blend ten yellow over ripened bananas
Pour mixture into a bowl
Add 8 oz. of rice flour
Add four tablespoons of brown sugar
Add a half teaspoon of nutmeg and a pinch of cinnamon
Slowly stir the mixture for a consistent batte free of lumps
(Note: Do not use a blender for this. If the mixture is too smooth the akara balls will loose their crunchy taste)
Remember, the mixture needs to be just right, not too thick or thin, to allow for the proper formation of the akara ball
Place two cups of olive or vegetable oil in a 10 inch frying pan and heat under medium fire for five to ten minutes
Using your fingers, scoop up a small portion of the blended mixture and release in the forms of balls into the hot oil
Repeat this step until the pot is full with akara balls
If you prefer, use a teaspoon to assist you until you become accustomed to using your fingers
Using a fork control the balls of rice akara as they cook to a brown colors
Revmove from the pan and place on a plate and allow to cool for five to ten minutes

Serves approximately 10 people

Sauce for Rice and Beans Akara

Ingredients

1. Onions
2. Sweet peppers
3. Thyme
4. Black Pepper
5. Seasoned salt
6. Tomato paste
7. Olive or Vegetable oil
8. All purpose seasoning
9. Hot pepper
   (Habenero or Cayenne)

Preparation

Place a 10 inch skillet on the stove
Add two cups of olive or vegetable oil, turn heat to low flame (this is to prevent the oil from overheating)
Chop and blend four onions and two sweet peppers with one cup of water and add slowly into the pot with oil
Add one tablespoon of black pepper and all purpose seasoning
Add two tablespoons of seasoned salt and a half teaspoon of salt
Add a half teaspoon of thyme
Add three teaspoons of tomato paste
Stir ingredients in the pot into an even mix and cook for 15-20 minutes
Taste as you cook to ensure proper seasoning
If a spicy sauce is preferred, add one habanero or a half teaspoon of cayenne pepper
Stir consistently as it cooks for another 10-15 minutes under a low to medium heat untill sauce starts to sizzle
Fry for two to three minutes and turn the heat off
Cook with your heart and listen to your instincts

The Dining Table

An Awujoh Feast

Food often becomes the center of many celebrations. As I said earlier good food is most times the hallmark of a festive occasion. The delicious tastes and smells of any one dish can leave an indellible mark on one's mind. As friends and family members unite around good food so can adversaries if only for a short while.

An awujoh feast in Sierra Leone displays a variety of dishes that most times represent most if not all of a host's favorite dishes. Awujoh (Ahh-woo-joe) is a Yuroba word from Nigeria that means "a festive gathering". In Sierra Leone an Awujoh feast usually celebrates the commemoration of a dearly departed loved one.

Like the Sierra Leone salad also known as African salad, that is shown to the right side featuring the eggs. An Awujoh feast unites different flavors, dishes, colors, aromas, friends and family members in an eclectic blend that is only African.

Pehpeh Chicken

Pehpeh chicken is a delicacy in Sierra Leone that is indigenous to other parts of the West coast of Africa. Its name is directly attributed to the fiery nature of the peppers that enhance this dish. An awesome blend of seasonings herbs and spices create a mouth watering delight that is only described as delicious.

Ingredients

1. Chicken
2. Peanut butter
3. Lemon Juice
4. Onions
5. Sweet peppers
6. Tomato paste
7. Hot peppers
   (Habenero or Cayenne)
8. Black pepper
9. All purpose seasoning
10. Seasoned Salt
11. Salt
12. Garlic powder

Preparation

Cut up a whole chicken into parts as desired
Wash with lime and water; dry off all excess water
Add two tablespoons of seasoned salt and black pepper
Add one tablespoon of all purpose seasoning and garlic powder
Add a half teaspoon of salt, rub seasonings throughout the chicken
Let the chicken marinate for two hours
For best results, cook on a charcoal grille
Keep the grille covered to ensure slow cooking and a true absorption of the smoke flavor into the chicken. This gives a delicious smoked flavor
Cook until finished (Hint: Keep chicken moist by turning the pieces over at 15-20 minutes intervals and flip no more than twice on the grille) Avoid puncturing of chicken skin as you cook
If chaecoal grille is not available,cook in an oven at 375 degrees for   75-90 minutes

Preparation of Suace

Chop two onions and one sweet pepper then place in blender
Add one habanero pepper (if a spicier sauce is desired)
Add two two tablespoon of tomoto paste and a half teaspoon of salt
Add one tablespoon of season salt, garlic powder, all purpose seasoning
Add three tablespoons of lemon juice
Add one 9 oz. bottle of ceamy peanut butter
Add one cup of wate and blend
Pour blended mixture into a 6 quart sauce pot and cook under a low to medium fire stirring consistently as it cooks
Cook for 15-20 minutes or until sauce is thick
If the mixture gets too thick, add 1/4 cup of water to thin as desired
Pour the peanut butter sauce generously over the chicken or apply with a brush
Place chicken coveed with sauce in an uncoveed pan, place pan in oven for 5-10 minutes
Serve with salad or jollof rice
Serves approximately 2 people

Cassava Bread and Fry Fish

The most crucial aspect of this dish is the seasoning of the fish. Anyone can fry fish however, the seasoning process is what gives the fish in this dish its true essence. Crispy on the outside while flaky on the inside, tasty down to the bone.

Ingredients

1. Croaker Fish or Tilapia Fish
2. Cassava Bread
3. Onions
4. Olive or vegetable oil
5. Seasoned Salt
6. Salt
7. Black pepper
8. Tomato paste
9. Garlic powder
10. Thyme
11. Water

NOTE: Use fillet fish if you are concerned about bones

Preparation of fish

Use a medium size cleaned whole fish and place in a bowl of water
Add two tablespoons of lime juice and soak for 1 minute and rinse
Slice two cuts into the flish down to the bone, on both sides
Add one teaspoon of season salt, black pepper and garlic powder
Rub seasonings into the fish
Place a 12 inch frying skillet on a medium to low fire
Add 2 cups of olive or vegetable oil and heat for 2-3 minutes
Place the fish in skillet, fry each side for three to five minutes or until crispy
Remove fish from pan and place on a plate to cool

Preparation of cassava bread

Place one dried cassava bread on a plate
Sprinkle cassave bread with water to moisten evenly
Do not over saturate with water
Place the cassava bread in a microwave for two to three minutes
An oven can also be used at 250 degrees for five to ten minutes

Preparation of Sauce

Place an 8 inch skillet on the stove
Add one cup of olive or vegetable oil under low flame
Chop and blend one onion and sweet pepper with a half cup of water and add slowly into the pan with oil
Add one tablespoon black pepper and seasoned salt
Add one half teaspoon salt, garlic powder and thyme
Add one tablespoon tomato paste and stir ingredients in pot evenly
Cook for 15-20 minutes and taste as you cook
Slice one onion and sweet pepper into long strips
Once sauce begins to fry, add the sliced onions and sweet pepper
Stir at intervals as it cooks for approximately five to ten minutes
Serve the fish, cassava bread and sauce together as shown

Serves one to two people

Attieke
Achekeh/Soak Gari

Acheke is indigenous to the Ivory coast. Over time with travelers crossing over boundaries and settling in new areas through out Africa, Acheke has found its way to the dinner table in Sierra Leone and other parts of West Africa. Due to the softness and almost weightlessness of the grains, Acheke is a flavorful and satisfying dish.

Ingredients

1. Croaker Fish or Tilapia Fish (whole or fillet fish)
2. Gari
3. Onions
4. Olive or vegetable oil
5. Seasoned Salt
6. Salt
7. Black pepper
8. Tomato paste
9. Garlic powder
10. Thyme
11. Water
12. Sweet peppers

Preparation of fish
Use a medium size cleaned whole fish, rinse with water and lime juice
Remove excess moisture from fish
Slice two cuts into fish on both sides
Add one teaspoon of seasoned salt, black pepper, garlic powder
Rub seasonings into the fish
Place a 12 inch skillet on a medium to low fire
Add two cups of olive or vegetable oil and heat for two to three minutes
Place fish in skillet, fry each side for three to five minutes or until crispy

Preparation of Sauce
Place an 8 inch skillet on the stove
Add 1/4 cup of olive or vegetable oil under low flame
Slice two onions and two sweet peppers then add to pot
Add one tablespoon of black pepper and seasoned salt
Add one half teaspoon of salt, garlic powder and thyme
Add one tablespoon of tomato paste and stir ingredients in pot
Cook for 10-15 minutes or until onions are tender
Taste as you cook and spinkle a tablespoon of water as you cook

Preparation of Acheke
Place two cups of gari in a bowl and lightly wet gari by sprinkling a little bit of water at a time to make it moist but not soaking wet
Using a large spoon, mix the moist gari around the bowl to evenly spread the moistue and make the gari soft
Add one tablespoon of seasoned salt and continue to mix gari
Place a 12 inch skillet on stove under low fire add two tablespoons of oil
Pour the moist gari mixture into the skillet and immediately start to mix the grains with a large spoon to distribute the heat and soften grains Sprinkle water as you mix for ensure adequate softness of grains.
This process should not take more than three to five minutes
Place cooked gari on a plate, add fish and ganish with sauce

Serves approximtely 2-3 people

Scotch Eggs

A colorful and tasty blend of ground beef and boiled eggs. A delicious appetizer or snack that can only excite your guests and create a memorable occasion.

Ingredients

1. Eggs
2. Ground beef
3. Salt
4. Black pepper
5. Seasoned salt
6. Garlic powder
7. Bread crumbs
8. Onions
9. Sweet peppers

Preparation

Preheat the oven to 350 degrees
Place 12 eggs in a pot of water and boil for about 8-10 minutes
Peel eggs and place in a bowl
Chop two onions and two sweet peppers then place in a blender
Add a half teaspoon of salt
Add one tablespoon of seasoned salt, black pepper and garlic powder
Add 1/4 cup of water and blend
Place two pounds of ground beef in a bowl, add blended mixture
Mix the blended mixture into the ground beef to ensure a wholesome blend of ground beef and the mixture
Mold ground beef around each individual egg by wrapping the beef with your hands around the hard boiled eggs
Pour some bread crumbs into a bowl
Crack and whip two eggs in a separate bowl
Carefully dip the molded ground beef and eggs into the whipped eggs and then into the bread crumbs making sure that each wrap is evenly covered with bread crumbs
Place in a baking pan lightly covered with cooking spay
Put in the pre-heated oven and bake for 30-45 minutes or until golden brown.
Turn scotch eggs over at 15 minutes intervals
Remove from oven, allow to cool for 5-10 minutes
Cut in quarters and serve

Serve 20-24 people

African Salad

Sierra Leone Salad

This is one of the wonders of Africa. The vibrant colors of its various ingredients combine in an eclectic array that is invitingly delicious. This Salad eats like a meal.

Ingredients

1. Lettuce
2. Boiled Eggs
3. Onions
4. Carrots
5. Canned Pink Salmon
6. Vegetable Salad
7. Baked beans
8 Spam/Luncheon meat
9. Cucumber
10. Salad dressing
11. Tomatoes

Note: Any salad dressing is okay but salad cream dressing is commonly used.

Preparation

Start by boiling six eggs nice and hard
Wash, dry and cut two bunchs of green leaf lettuce and place on a serving plate
Slice one onion and mix into leaves
Add two shaved carrots
Slice one whole cucumber and add to plate
Slice two tomatoes and spread on top of the salad
Take one can of Spam/Luncheon meat, slice into thin pieces and add evenly on top of the salad
Open can of pink salmon, remove skin and bones
Place chunks of salmon evenly on top of the salad
Add one can of baked beans
Add one can of vegetable salad
Peel and slice the boiled eggs into thin slices
Add sliced eggs to the salad

Serves approximately 10-12 people

Foofoo

Cassava starch

A staple to most west African regions, foofoo is sometimes referred to as gari, cassava starch, and yucca. Foofoo is also sometimes called eba which is totally different but also derivd from cassava. Foofoo compliments most palavasauces. It tastes best when eaten with your hands.

Depending on what part of Africa you come from, the preparation of foofoo varies. Our methods describe a process that is simple and refined utilizing mordern technology. The original process throughout most of Africa is done by using a Mataodoo and a Mata pencil also known as a mortar bucket and a mortar pencil in places like Jamaica.

Ingredients

1. Frozen Foofoo (Cassava or Yucca)
2. Lemon
3. Water

Preparation

Thaw a packet of frozen foofoo/cassava/ yucca in a bowl
Blend cuts of foofoo/cassava/ yucca with half a cup of water into a fine puree
Squeeze one lemon into the mixture
Allow to sit for about 24 hours
Drain the water and impurities that float to the top without losing the saturated mix at the bottom of the container
Do this process for four to five days and the foofoo is now ready to be cooked
(This is the process to prepare the pre-cooked foofoo. A fast solution is to search for ready to cook foofoo in an African market and follow the steps below to cook)
Place mixture in an open 6 quart saucepan under low fire
Stir the mixture in the pot as it cooks making sure that all the lumps are removed as it cooks
As the mixture thickens, loosen the consistency by adding 1/4 cup of water at a time, while continuously stiring until the mixture is completely cooked
More water creates a thin loose mix. Less water creates a thick and hearty mixture
Using a large cooking spoon to remove portions of the mixture from the pot, wet a flat dish and place the spoon of foofoo mixture on the wet dish
Using your bare hands, slightly wet and mold the foofoo mixture into a ball
One packet of fofoo should make about 4-6 balls
Serve with any palava suace or groundnut soup

Shakpah
Sorrell Pods

A seasonal Palavasauce cooked with egusi. It is mouth watering, delicious, tasty and flavorful. Shakpah can be eaten with foofoo, rice or eba. Like most other palava sauce Shakpah can be made with or without palm oil.

Ingredients

1. Shakpah
2. Palm Oil
3. Smoked Fish
   (Barracuda, Kinney or Stalk Fish)
4. Grated Egusi seeds
5. Hot peppers
   (Habanero or cayenne)
6. Water
7. Seasoned salt
8. All purpose seasoning
9. Black pepper
10. Boullion cubes
11. Onions
12. Sweet peppers
13, Beef, Chicken, Pork or Fish as preferred

Preparation

Place two 16 oz. packets of shakpah pods in a bowl and cover with boiling hot water for five to ten minutes
Pour into a strainer, rub and rinse twice in cold water to remove the sour taste
Place a 12 quart saucepan on the stove
Add four cups of water and two cups of palm oil and bring to a boil
Chop and blend six onions, three sweet peppers with a half cup of water
Add the mixture to the pot
Add a half teaspoon of salt
Add two tablespoons of black pepper
Add one tablespoon of all purpose seasoning
Add two tablespoons of seasoned salt and two boullion cubes
Take two Kinney or one chunk of Barracuda fish, remove skin and bones, rinse and add the dried fish to the pot
Cover the pot and let it continue to boil for 15-20 mnutes
Add meats as desired within additional fifteen minuets of boiling
(Note: Beef takes longer to tenderize than chicken. Pay close attention to the tenderness of your meats and remove meats if desired tenderness is acquired)
Now cover the pot and continue to cook under a medium to high flame for 15-20 minutes
Depending on your tolerance for heat add hot peppers
Stir consistently as you cook while observing the sauce in the pot to obtain a smooth and fine taste of the leaves
Add three 8 oz. packets of grated egusi to the pot and lower the fire
Add prepared Shakpah pods to the pot
Allow the mixture to cook for at least 20-25 minutes while stirring consistently to ensure adequate balance of spices until the dish is thick
Serve over white rice or foofoo, eba or gari

Serves approximately 8-10 people

Sawa Sawa

As the name implies through its pronunciation Sawa Sawa directly translated means Sour Sour. Emulched in the herbs and spices and the touch of good hands these leaves create a compelling argument for preference at the dinner table.

A hint of sour taste compounded with the flavor of palm oil strategically balanced by herbs seasonings and the smoky flavor of Barracuda fish. No palm oil, then its Whate/White Sawa Sawa. Use Palm oil then its red Sawa Sawa. Africa never tasted so good.

Ingredients

1. Sawa Sawa
2. Palm Oil
3. Smoked Fish
   (Barracuda, Kinney or Stalk   Fish)
4. Grated Egusi seeds
5. Hot peppers
   (Habanero or cayenne)
6. Water
7. Seasoned salt
8. All purpose seasoning
9. Black pepper
10. Boullion cubes
11. Onions
12. Sweet peppers
13, Beef, Chicken, Pork or Fish as
    preferred

Preparation

Place two 16 oz. packets of Sawa Sawa leaves in a bowl and cover with boiling hot water for five to ten minutes
Pour into a strainer, rub and rinse twice in cold water to remove the sour taste
Place a 12 quart saucepan on the stove
Add four cups of water and two cups of palm oil and bring to a boil
Chop and blend six onions, three sweet peppers with a half cup of water
Add the mixture to the pot
Add a half teaspoon of salt
Add two tablespoons of black pepper
Add one tablespoon of all purpose seasoning
Add two tablespoons of seasoned salt and two boullion cubes
Take two Kinney or one chunk of Barracuda fish, remove skin and bones, rinse and add the dried fish to the pot
Cover the pot and let it continue to boil for 15-20 mnutes
Add meats as desired within additional fifteen minuets of boiling
(Note: Beef takes longer to tenderize than chicken. Pay close attention to the tenderness of your meats and remove meats if desired tenderness is acquired)
Now cover the pot and continue to cook under a medium to high flame for 15-20 minutes
Depending on your tolerance for heat add hot peppers
Stir consistently as you cook while observing the sauce in the pot to obtain a smooth and fine taste of the leaves
Add three 8 oz. packets of grated egusi to the pot and lower the fire
Add prepared Sawa Sawa leaves to the pot
Allow the mixture to cook for at least 20-25 minutes while stiring consistently to ensure adequate balance of spices until the dish is thick
Serve over white rice or foofoo, eba or gari

Serves approximately 8-10 people

Nutritional Properties of Basic Ingredients

Palm Oil

It is a myth that Palm oil is not nutritionally good for consumption. This is scientifically undocumented and is just an unfounded rumor that is spread even amongst Africans. Palm oil has very good nutritional properties that have been scientifically researched and documented by organizations like American Palm Oil Council (**APOC**), and the Malaysian Palm oil council (**MPOC**). The following facts were stated by the **APOC**. Palm oil is not Palm kernel oil or coconut oil. Palm oil is from the fruit of the palm tree commonly known in Sierra Leone, as Banga. Palm oil is physically and chemically different from palm kernel oil which is derived from the seed, and coconut oil, both of which are highly saturated. Palm oil has been a safe and nutritious source of edible oil for healthy humans for thousands of years.

Palm oil and its liquid fraction, palm olien are consumed worldwide as cooking oils and as constituents of margarines and shortenings. These oils are also incorporated into fat blends used in the manufacturing of a variety of food products as well as in home food preparation. Palm oil is cholesterol free and like most vegetable oils, Palm oil has a moderate level of saturation. It does not require hydrogenation for use as a fat component in foods and therefore does not contain trans fatty acids. Palm oil is rich in cartenoids, red(unprocessed) and red or golden (specially refined) palm oils. The major cooking oils in many parts of the world are rich sources of beta-carotene, a precursor of Vitamin A which some studies have found to have antioxidant properties. Palm oil products are naturally occurring sources of the antioxidant vitamin E constituents, tocopherols and tocotreinols. These natural antioxidants may act as scavengers of damaging oxygen free radicals. Some studies have suggested that antioxidants may play a protective role in cellular aging, atherosclerosis and cancer. Human feeding studies and epidemiologic data have found that Palm oil and Palm olien have effects on blood cholesterol that are similar to olive oils. In several studies of normocholesterolemic men and women, a diet that included Palm oil resulted in reduced blood cholesterol.

According to the APOC in an article entitled "The truth about Palm oil", it is stated that "Palm oil is a vegetable oil, not an animal oil or dairy product and therefore does not contain cholesterol" According to an article entitled "Tropical traditions" retrieved from www.tropicaltraditions.com, Palm oil in its natural state is a great source of carotenes which is a noted precursor to Vitamin A and tocotrienols (Vitamin E). Over time the use of Palm oil has dwindled even among some Africans because of myths and unsubstantiated representations about Palm oil. Among these myths are issues of high cholesterol, heart disease, increased blood sugars, obesity and bad circulation. These unfounded issues have led some Africans to create Palm oil based dishes with substitute oils that may in fact lack the healthy ingredients that Palm oil naturally posses.

In an article circulated by the APOC, Palm oil was noted to be an essential fatty acid-sufficient tropical oil that raises plasma cholesterol only when an excess of dietary cholesterol is presented in the diet (APOC, 2003). In the same article the world wide use of Palm oil was proclaimed and reference was made to palm oil lowering plasma cholesterol. Palm oil has been used in food preparation for over 5,000 years (APOC, 2003). Throughout the world Palm oil is used as an ingredient in various foods for coloring, flavor, cooking oil, margarine and shortening. According to the article " My Palm oil", the essence of Palm oil is seen everyday in our toothpaste, moisturizers for our skins, hotdogs at fast food restaurants and public buses that run on biodiesel. In Malaysia, Palm oil is called God's gift to mankind. Globally Palm oil is known as the most used domestic oil in the world. Here in the United States as the tensions and unfounded myths about Palm oil are negated by scientific facts that are mirrored by its use all over the world, Palm oil is becoming more sought after since the lifting of restrictions and proposed sanctions against the oil's use in 1994 by the U.S. FDA. The FDA announced the removal of restrictive labeling of Palm oil in 1994 (APOC, 2003). Palm oil is a major ingredient in most African dishes. We urge the reader to research and explore the oil's scientific facts and those mentioned here to make wise decisions that are based on facts and not hear say.

Cayenne Pepper

Cayenne pepper is a medicinal and nutritional herb. It is a high source of vitamin A and C. It has the complete B complex and is very rich in organic calcium and potassium which is one of the reasons it is good for the heart. In Sierra Leone, cayenne pepper is believed by the elders to rid the body of unwanted toxins. The actual scientific properties were never documented as it is today. "Recent clinical studies have been conducted on many of the old-time health applications for this miracle herb. Again and Again, the therapeutic value of Cayenne pepper has been medically validated". (Dr. Patrick Quillin- The Healing Power of Cayenne Pepper) Many herbalists believe that Cayenne pepper is the most useful and valuable herb in the herb kingdom. According to these herbalists this is true for the entire digestive system and the heart and circulatory system. Cayenne pepper has been noted to act as a catalyst and increases the effectiveness of other herbs when used with them. (Shirley's wellness Café.com)

Okra

According to medical studies Okra has several properties. The superior fiber found in Okra helps to stabilize blood sugar by curbing the rate at which sugar is absorbed from the intestinal tract. Okra's mucilage binds cholesterol and bile acid. Okra helps lubricate the large intestine due to its bulk laxative qualities. The okra fiber absorbs water and ensures bulk stools. This helps prevent and improve constipation. Okra assures the easy passage of waste from the body. Okra is non-toxic, has no adverse side effects, and is full of nutrients. Okra is easily accessible and economically affordable.

Habanero peppers

While peppers are known for their heat in foods, used improperly peppers can in most cases hinder the true taste of a dish. However used soulfully, peppers can enhance the taste and fullness of most dishes. When cooking with peppers one must take into account the tolerance of one's audience, the balance needed between ingredients that can heighten the taste while allowing for a palatable experience. Peppers are an important ingredient like all the other spices that collaborate to increase flavor, taste and health. Researchers are increasingly looking to natural options like Habanero peppers in the fight against cancer. Recent studies and trials demonstrated that capsaicin (a component found in Habanero peppers) has the ability to drive prostate cancer cells to act against themselves. This process in the article entitled "Last stage Cancer" is called apoptosis. The same reaction is suspected in like ingredients such as Jalapeño peppers. Further studies were noted to show a decrease in tumor sizes in laboratory rats of up to 80% reduction attributed to apoptosis.

Sweet potato leaves

Sweet potato leaves are used in the cooking of Potato leaves. However in its absence within the United States and other areas, spinach leaves are sometimes substituted. Sweet potato leaves provide dietary source of vitamins, minerals, antioxidants, dietary fiber and essential fatty acids (Johnson, 2010). These leaves have been scientifically proven to promote immune functions, reduce cardiovascular disease risk and suppress cancer cell growth (Johnson, 2010). According to scientists, research of the vegetables consumption have documented the potential of increased cardio protection and anti inflammatory and soothing properties. This heart shaped creeping vegetable is rich in beta carotene which is a major anti oxidant. In addition sweet potato leaves are rich in magnesium, zinc and vitamin B complex which are essential in the cure of arthritis.

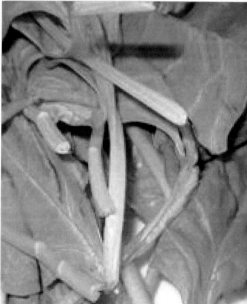

Bitter Leaves

Bitter leaves are common throughout West Africa. Depending on the locale it goes by different names. In Nigeria alone it has three different names that we are aware of. It is called onugbo by the Igbo tribe, ewuro by the Yoruba tribe and shiwaka by the Hausa tribe. In Sierra Leone it is called Bitter leaf. The leaf is known for multiple healing properties that span from diabetes, prostate cancer, malaria etc... Not too much scientific analysis is available on the vegetables properties. However throughout West Africa the leaf is known for its taste and dominance in treating and counteracting the affects of diabetes and other diseases. According to an article by The University of Texas, Bitter leaf extract may prevent or delay breast cancer and diabetes (Anonymous, 2005). According to this same article the famous chewing stick in Nigeria mostly used by the Hausa peoples, comes from the back of the root of the Bitter leaf plant. Its use as a chewing stick is vital to dental hygiene,

Cassava Leaves (Saka Saka/Mpondu)

Cassava leaves are rich in beta carotene, protein and vitamins B-12, B2 and Niacin. According to an article entitled "The healing properties of Cassava", Native American Indians have long used cassava leaves for medicinal purposes. Cassava in supplement form is effective in the fight against diarrhea, inflammation of all types of bruises and ulcers (Mays, 2007). In West Africa the leaves and the root of the plant are both utilized in numerous ways for dietary purposes. The Cassava root aka yucca or manioc is used to make gari, attieke/acheke, foofoo and eba. In its grated and fermented form it is known as gari. From its processed state as gari cassava is used to make attieke and eba. The actual root skinned and blended or pounded with a mixture of water and processed in a cleansing mixture of lime is eventually cooked to derive foofoo. Different types of cassava have varying levels of starch. The cassava root is a good source of carbohydrates.

Egusi

Egusi seeds are melon seeds that are well known through out West Africa and other parts. The seeds according to documented scientific analysis contain oils, protein fiber and carbohydrates. Further breakdown in the analysis of the seed's oil shows that it contains mostly oleic acids and linoleic acids. According to an article in Food Science Journal, Egusi seeds are a good source for essential amino acids, especially aginine, tryptophan and methionine (Simmons, 2006). Egusi according to the article also contains vitamins B1, B2, niacin, iron, zinc, potassium etc... (Simmons, 2006).

Scientific facts point to the importance of maintaining a good balance of linoleic acid (Omega 6faty acids) for help to fight against problems that include hair loss, dry hair, poor wound healing (Anonymous, nd). Oleic acids on the other hand have the potential of lowering total cholesterol level and raise levels of high density lipoproteins (HDLs) while lowering low density lipoproteins (LDLs) which are also known as bad cholesterol (wisegeek.com, nd.).

Global Connections and Influences

As we look at other cuisines and cultures throughout the world it is apparent that other ethnic cuisines are similar and sometimes identical to most African dishes. For example the Spanish rice resembles the African Jollof rice. Other items include the Spanish mondongo soup which is very much like the African Pehpeh soup. The manner in which they are prepared, the choice and use of various ingredients, the meats and produce used in the preparation of both items stories similarity and influence.

Spanning across to the Americas, dishes currently in the Gullah islands and cultural practices from their red rice to Africa's Jollof rice denote similarities and references that point to the practices of slaves and travelers that possess a common trait that is African. Historic facts document that the Gullah people are direct descendants of freed slaves brought to the now called Gullah islands from Senegal, Sierra Leone and Angola.

These slaves were brought to these Islands especifically for their knowledge in farming rice swamplands in the regions of these islands (Anonymous, 2000). The Jambalaya dish in Louisiana which derives its name from gumbo which means okra correlates to the Okra soup which usually consists of a medley of fish, beef, chicken and mixed spices. A further look at Portuguese dishes like paella, Louisiana's Jambalaya dish highly resembles the Jollof rice when it is cooked as "Wan Pot" which simply means every ingredient blended together in one pot. This notion also dates back to the slave trade where scraps and leftovers were utilized skillfully and stretched to make sustaining meals.

In Brazil the streets are lined with Acaraje which are similar to Akara balls and Puff puffs that line the streets of most West African countries. As I stated earlier there is a strong connection between African, Spanish, Portuguese, Indian and American soul cuisines that I believe dates back to the trans Atlantic slave trade. This connection is most times misunderstood because we inherently do not observe and relate the relocation of the ancestry lines of various ethnic groups as they were displaced and or migrated to different parts of the world.

These relationships are further evident in the use of common ingredients under varying names across the continents. For example Cassava also known as Manioc or Saka Saka is used to produce Gari, Attieke/Achecke, Tapioca, Eba, foofoo, cassava flour and bami. Gari, Attieke and foofoo are staples in the Ivory Coast, Sierra Leone, Ghana, Nigeria and other West African countries. Bami which also is quite close in preparation to Acheke is a staple in the West Indies (especially Jamaica).

The same Bami aka Cassava bread as it is known in Sierra Leone and parts of South America and Santa Domingo is used in almost the same ways with fish and seafood among the various cultures. The plain cassava root is boiled, fried or baked in several dishes in India, Africa and Spanish speaking countries.

Until the foods of Africa are scientifically analyzed without political bias and misrepresentation the ingredients of Africa's cuisines will continue to go unnoticed and unutilized in promoting healthier life styles.

Summary

African foods and their ingredients have made Africans healthy for over 5,000 years. Its time we recognize the true facts of its attributes and position it in our daily menus. I believe that African foods like all other cuisines has its strong points and its weak points. Any diet must be accompanied with regular exercise, good medical monitoring and keen awareness of the foods attributes. It is my hope that the facts mentioned in this book will begin a meaningful dialogue and bring increased awareness to a cuisine that has long served to promote healthy lifestyles throughout Africa and other continents.

The name for most of African sauces is called Palava sauce or Plasas. According to the Oxford dictionary the word Palava originated from Portugal which means to speak aloud.

In West Africa, mainly Sierra Leone in the creole language Palava or Plabah) means to argue or quarrel.

A look at the Palava sauce pot displays a soulful arrangement that can be seen as an argument of exotic vegetables, palm oil, spices, seasonings, meats and fish that I feel are shouting aloud for a chance at the dinner table. It is time to make a delicious noise with these dishes that can only promote healthier lifestyles. We must look past the myths to see the facts of this cuisine's attributes.

References

Anonymous, (2005), Bitter Leaf Extract... Health, Retrieved March 13, 2011, from http://www.utexas.edu/conferences/afric a/ade/1261.html

V.S. Dennis, (2005), what is Palava, Retrieved on February 05, 2011, from http://www.phrases.org.UK/bulletin_boar d/41/messages/496html

American Palm Oil Council, (nd.), Your Vegetable for better health, retrieved from http://www.americanpalmoil.com

Anonymous, (2009), Prostrate and pancreatic cancer-Habanero peppers too hot to handle, retrieved December 21, 2009 from http://www.lateststagecancer.com/2009/ 12/prostrate-cancer-habernero-peppers-too-hot-to-handle.html

Anonymous, (2005), Bitter Leaf extract may prevent, delay breast cancer, diabetes, healthy, Retrieved from http://www.utexas.edu/conferences/afric a/ads/1261.html

Anonymous (nd.) Gullah History, Retrieved March 2009, from http://www.islandpacket.com/man/gullah/ history.html

O.M.Oluba, et.al. (2008), Physiochemical properties of fatty acid composition of Citrullus Ianatus (Egusi Melon) seed oil, Retrieved January 05, 2011, from http://www.britannica.com/bps/additional content/18/35705193

Anonymous, (2008), the health benefit of Bitter leaf, retrieved February 04, 2010 from www.nairaland.com/nigeria/topic-158681.0.html

J.M. Pace, (2010), Sweet Potato Leaves, Retrieved January 10, 2010 from http://www.ncbi.nlm.nih.gov/pubmed/208 83418

Anonymous, (2007), Peanut Butter, retrieved from http://www.peanut-butter.org/peanut-butter/Health+Benefits+of+peanut+Butter#

Anonymous (nd.), Virgin Red Palm Oil, Retrieved from http://www.tropicaltraditions.com/red_pal m_oil htm? gclid=CLrgt

Dedication

In life one meets a lot of teachers. My first and most influential teachers were my Mother the late Gifty Jane John and my father the late Rev G. Ademu-John. My good fortune as a student of good African cuisine was to learn from one of Africa's finest teachers, my wife Rita Ademu-John. She exposed the depth and realm of soul cooking to me.

Rita taught me the joys of cooking the African way. She showed me how to listen to the pot. Through her I relized that there is a timing and precision that comes with practice, patience and perseverance. In her unique way she guided my senses to fully comprehend the ultimate balance of delicious cooking that is usually described in Africa by the essence of a chef's hands.

My wife has one of the finest hands in African cooking which she got from her mother, my friend and fan of my cooking the Late Pricess Cole.

This cookbook is designed to stage some of Africa's most precious jewels that continue to go unnoticed. African cuisine is quite delicious and holds numerous healing properties that are currently being revealed through researchers and fans.

About the Author

Shikaorsor Ademu-John was born in Freetown Sierra Leone, West Africa. He attended the Methodist Boys High School and then traveled to The United States of America to further his studies in Architectural design and technology. In America he attended the Institute of Design and Construction, The New York Institute of Technology and the City University of New York. He later attended Ashford University for Graduate studies in Healthcare administration.

Shika's life experiences include a combination of sales, business ownership and management. He is active in his church community The United Methodist Church of New Brunswick, New Jersey. He is a proud father of three sons Shika Jr., Justin and Kevin. His lifelong partner, friend and love of over 32 years is Rita Ademu-John. Together they founded the Awujoh restaurant that was located in Franklin Township of Somerset, New Jersey. His love for African cuisine and customer requests from the restaurant launched this cookbook, My Wife's Hands.

My Wife's Hands is an African cookbook that is designed to stage some of Africa's most precious jewels that continue to go unnoticed. African cuisine is quite delicious and holds numerous healing properties that are presently being revealed through researchers and fans. The book offers a pictorial thesis that is accompanied with detailed recipes which unveil the secrets, methods and essence of African cooking. The measure of a chef's ability and creativity is defined by his or her hands. The book's website (www.awujoh.com) may offer periodically, short videos and digital displays of both African life and a visual presentation of the preparation of some of the book's recipes.

Acknowledgements

It is said that a picture is worth a thousand words. On that note I would like to express my deep gratitude to Marc Skinner for his skillful eye and precision in documenting the vibrant colors and accents of the various dishes that he photographed.

To my fans especially Aunty Cho, Mrs. Juliana Rowe and my late Aunty Jeredine. Together with all our customers at Awujoh restaurant and our catering fans a special thank you for your words of encouragement that served to make this cookbook a reality.

To my sons Shika Jr, Justin and Kevin for your assistance. To my wife Rita, I can never thank you enough for your patience and encouragement through it all. Your support and understanding have been a strong foundation. I thank God for you.

To my Savior and Heavenly Father all praise, honor and glory to you.

In God all things are possible.

Thank you for embarking on this journey with us, we hope that you enjoyed a taste of Afirca.
For more tips, recipes and instructional videos on African cooking you can refer to
www.awujoh.com

We look forward to cooking with you again